PREFACE

This study analyzes the major proposals put forward since World War II to reorganize the reserve components of the Army (Army Reserve and Army National Guard), Air Force (Air Force Reserve and Air National Guard), Navy, and Marine Corps. These proposals encompass efforts to merge the reserve components (with other reserve components or with their respective active services) and to rebalance capabilities between reserve and active components. This study includes a review of both the legislation, proposed and enacted, that accompanied the proposals initiated by the military and the relevant congressional committee hearings and reports. A timeline of major actions/events accompanies this narrative. The report also includes a list of titles and sections of the U.S. Code that would require amendment in order to effect a merger of the Army National Guard with the Army Reserve and the Air National Guard with the Air Force Reserve.

I0455425

TABLE OF CONTENTS

TABLES

INTRODUCTION

Throughout the post–World War II period, the National Guard and Reserves have maintained separate identities despite periodic proposals to merge both reserve components. The two most serious proposals came in 1947, when the so-called Gray Board convened by Secretary of Defense James Forestall to examine the status of reserve forces recommended the abolition of the National Guard, and in 1964, when Secretary of Defense Robert McNamara recommended merging all reserve components of the army under the management of the National Guard. Both proposals failed because of strong congressional opposition, fueled by the effective lobbying of associations affiliated with the National Guard and Reserves and other interest groups. Since the introduction of the Total Force Policy in 1973, reserve forces have been increasingly integrated with active-duty forces, to the extent that the distinction between the two has begun to fade. Some observers argue that this integration has gone too far in view of the traditional citizen-soldier role of the National Guard and Reserves.

POST-WORLD WAR II LEGISLATION

Immediately following the end of World War II, Congress enacted two laws that affected the organizational structure and manpower strengths of the reserve components. In July 1947, Congress enacted Pub.L.No. 80–253, the National Security Act of 1947. Section 207 of this law established within the U.S. military a separate Department of the Air Force, defined to include all of its reserve components.[1] The law also stipulates that the National Guard Bureau shall,

> in addition to the functions and duties performed by it for the Department of the Army, be charged with similar functions and duties for the Department of the Air Force, and shall be the channel of communication between the Department of the Air Force and the several States on all matters pertaining to the Air National Guard.[2]

In June 1948, Congress enacted Pub.L.No. 80–759, the Selective Service Act of 1948, providing for the call-up of National Guard and other reserve component forces at the discretion of Congress or the president. Section 1 (d) of this law states as policy that

> it is essential that the strength and organization of the National Guard, both Ground and Air, as an integral part of the first line defenses of this Nation, be at

---

[1] Pub.L.No. 80–253, *National Security Act of 1947*, 61 Stat 495, 502, July 26, 1947.
[2] 61 Stat 495, 503.

all times maintained and assured. To this end, it is the intent of the Congress that whenever Congress shall determine that units and organizations are needed for the national security in excess of those of the Regular components of the Ground Forces and the Air Forces, and those in active service, the National Guard of the United States, both Ground and Air … together with such units of the Reserve components as are necessary for a balanced force, shall be ordered to active Federal service and continued therein so long as such necessity exists.[3]

Section 7 of Pub.L.No. 80–579 authorizes the president to "order into the active service of the armed forces of the United States," for a maximum of 21 consecutive months, members "of any or all reserve components of the armed forces of the United States who shall have had less than ninety days' continuous active service" in the armed forces, exclusive of periods of active training duty.[4]

THE GRAY BOARD (IMMEDIATE POST–WORLD WAR II ERA)

The first major official post–World War II study examining the status of reserve forces was the so-called Gray Board, which was named after its chairman, Assistant Secretary of the Army Gordon Gray. Secretary of Defense Forrestal convened this board in November 1947, and it presented a final report in June 1948.[5] The Gray Board recommended the merger of the National Guard and Reserves into a federally controlled force called the "National Guard of the United States."[6] This conclusion was based on the finding that the National Guard—with its dual state and federal allegiances—was not suitable for the Cold War. However, the National Guard and the National Guard Association of the United States successfully lobbied Congress against the Gray Board's recommendations.[7] The Gray Board also criticized reserve forces for being long on experience, but short on readiness. The reason for this critique was that many reservists were World War II veterans, who were resentful at being recalled to military service, while

---

[3] Pub.L.No. 80–759, *Selective Service Act of 1948*, 62 Stat 604, June 24, 1948.
[4] 62 Stat 604, 614.
[5] I.M. McQuiston, "History of the Reserves Since the Second World War," *Military Affairs*, 1953, 23–24.
[6] Michael D. Doubler, *Civilian in Peace, Soldier in War—The Army National Guard, 1636–2000* (Lawrence, Kansas: University Press of Kansas, 2003), 229.
[7] Doubler, 229.

younger men were able to pursue civilian careers.[8] Even though Secretary Forrestal convened the Gray Board, he did not endorse its recommendations.[9]

THE ARMED FORCES RESERVE ACT AND OTHER 1950s POLICIES (THE COLD WAR)

Although the Selective Service Act of 1948 provided a fresh flow of manpower into the reserves, readiness was an issue when the reserves were partially mobilized for the Korean conflict that erupted in 1950.[10] In response to some of the deficiencies with the Korean mobilization, Pub.L.No. 66–476, the Armed Forces Reserve Act of 1952, set out new policies for reserve forces.[11] Section 201 (a) of this act established as general policy that

> the reserve components of the Armed Forces of the United States are maintained for the purpose of providing trained units and qualified individuals to be available for active duty in the Armed Forces of the United States in time of war or national emergency, and at such other times as the national security may require, to meet the requirements of the Armed forces of the United States in excess of those of the Regular components thereof, during and after the period needed for procurement and training of additional trained units and qualified individuals to achieve the planned mobilization.[12]

Sections 202 and 204 of the act established seven reserve components (the National Guard of the United States, the Army Reserve, the Naval Reserve, the Marine Corps Reserve, the Air Force Reserve, the Air National Guard of the United States, and the Coast Guard Reserve) and three levels of reserves (ready, standby, and retired), of which the Ready Reserve had the highest priority.[13] Section 205 (b) authorized troop strength of 1.5 million for the Ready Reserve.[14] Individual guardsmen and reservists were given the opportunity to volunteer for active duty for routine, noncombat missions to avoid mobilization.[15]

---

[8] Abbott A. Brayton, "American Reserve Policies Since World War II," *Military Affairs*, no. 4 (1972): 140.
[9] "Assessing the Structure and Mix of Future Active and Reserve Forces: Final Report to the Secretary of Defense," RAND National Defense Research Institute, 1992, 26–27, http://www.rand.org/pubs/monograph_reports/MR140.2.
[10] Brayton, 140.
[11] Brayton, 140.
[12] Pub.L.No. 66–476, *Armed Forces Reserve Act of 1952*, 66 Stat 481, 482, July 1, 1952.
[13] Michael R. Thirtle, "A Brief Description of the U.S. Military" in "Educational Benefits and Officer-Commissioning Opportunities Available to U.S. Military Service Members," RAND, 2001, 73; 66 Stat 483.
[14] 66 Stat 483.
[15] Charles J. Gross, "A Chronological History of the Air National Guard and its Antecedents, 1908–2007," April 2, 2007, http://www.ngb.army.mil/features/AF60th/ANG-CHRON_1908_2007.doc.

In May and March 1952, respectively, the Reserve Officer Personnel Act (H.R. 7856, 82nd Congress) and the Armed Forces Equalization of Benefits Act (H.R. 7002, 82nd Congress) were introduced, but not enacted. The former would have provided reserve officers with promotion opportunities equal to those for active-duty officers. The latter would have provided them with equal benefits.[16] In 1957 the army for the first time required all newly enlisted reservists to complete at least four months of active-duty service, so that they would have the benefit of the same training as active-duty personnel.[17] However, an ongoing problem during the 1950s was that reserve units were not staffed to full manpower, despite congressional action in the form of the Reserve Forces Acts of 1952 and 1955.[18] The 1952 law set the maximum enrollment in the Ready Reserve at 1.5 million persons. Pursuant to the Reserve Forces Act of 1955, Pub.L.No. 84–305, the ceiling was raised to 2.9 million persons, and the president was authorized to call up as many as 1 million Ready Reservists in the case of a national emergency.[19] Under Section 2 (i) of Pub.L. No. 84–305, until August 1, 1959, "whenever the President determines that the enlisted strength of the Ready Reserve" of each of the reserve components "cannot be maintained at the level which he determines to be necessary in the interest of national defense," enlistments are authorized for up to 250,000 men ages 17 to 18½ for a period of eight years, including an initial three to six months of active duty.[20] In 1959 Congress sought to counter President Dwight D. Eisenhower's skepticism about the military value of the reserves by mandating a minimum force level of 700,000 troops.[21]

By 1960, all Army Reserve and National Guard divisions had been restructured into "pentomic" divisions, consisting of five fighting units, including one designed for tactical nuclear warfare.[22] This short-lived reorganization, which was reversed in the 1960s, was an outgrowth of Pub.L.No. 85–599, the Defense Reorganization Act of 1958.[23]

---

[16] McQuiston, 26.
[17] Brayton, 140.
[18] Brayton, 141.
[19] Pub.L.No. 84–305, 69 Stat 598, 599, August 9, 1955.
[20] 69 Stat 598, 600.
[21] U.S. Army Center of Military History, Office of the Chief of Military History, *American Military History* (chapter 26, "The Army and the New Look"), 591, http://www.army.mil/cmh-pg/books/amh/AMH-26.htm.
[22] U.S. Army Center of Military History, "The Army and the New Look," 585.
[23] Tom Donnelly, "The Force We Have," *Armed Forces Journal*, June 2006, http://www.armedforcesjournal.com/ 2006/06/1813581; Pub.L.No. 85–599, *Defense Reorganization Act of 1958*, 72; Stat 514, August 6, 1958.

RACIAL AND GENDER INTEGRATION

A nettlesome issue that required sustained attention throughout the post–World War II period was racial and gender integration. In July 1948, President Harry S. Truman ordered the integration of the armed forces in Executive Order No. 9981.[24] However, integration of the Army National Guard occurred slowly in many states, in part over the issue of state control. Only in 1965, following the Civil Rights Act of 1964 and controversial National Guard deployments during race riots and anti–Vietnam War protests, did the National Guard command threaten to withhold recognition from state units denying membership based on race.[25] Women achieved equal access to the National Guard in 1971–72.[26]

In the midst of heavy combat in Vietnam during 1965–70, the Army National Guard was involved primarily in maintaining civil order during race riots and antiwar demonstrations. Following National Guard deployments in the Watts section of Los Angeles in 1965 and in Detroit in 1967, President Lyndon Johnson appointed a National Advisory Commission on Civil Disorders, popularly known as the Kerner Commission after its chairman, Illinois Governor Otto Kerner, Jr.[27] In February 1968, the Kerner Commission published a report that called for the National Guard to undergo training for crowd control and urban fighting. The report cited the problem posed by a predominantly white force being asked to quell black rioters and encouraged the recruitment of minorities by the National Guard. The training came before widespread violence in 1968, when a total of 105,000 guardsmen were deployed in response to disturbances in 29 states and the District of Columbia.[28]

McNAMARA PROPOSALS (VIETNAM ERA)

In 1961 President John F. Kennedy called up reserve forces in response to the Berlin crisis. The resulting mobilization went smoothly and was generally regarded as successful because it had the effect of deterring war. One important individual who did not share the consensus view was Secretary of Defense Robert McNamara.[29]

---

[24] Doubler, 248; 13 Fed.Reg. 4311, July 28, 1948.
[25] Doubler, 249.
[26] Doubler, 249–50.
[27] Doubler, 263.
[28] Doubler, 263–64.
[29] "Assessing the Structure and Mix of Future Active and Reserve Forces," 30; Doubler, 251.

During his stormy tenure as secretary of defense during 1961–68, McNamara attempted a variety of efforts to reorganize reserve forces. In early 1962, McNamara proposed a plan that would eliminate four National Guard divisions and four Army Reserve divisions. In terms of unit and personnel strength, the plan would have eliminated 717 units (58,000 personnel) from an original force of 8,734 units (700,000 personnel). Of the 29 divisions remaining after the reorganization, six divisions would be high priority (ready to deploy within eight weeks), two divisions with special missions would be conventional priority (ready to deploy within 12 weeks), and 21 divisions would be low priority (ready to deploy within 20–34 weeks). However, the number of divisions is deceptive in that the six high-priority units, including support troops, would involve a force of 462,000, whereas the low-priority units would involve 180,000. Viewed this way, the total ready force would be reduced from 700,000 to 462,000. The initial and proposed reserve component structure is presented in the following charts (see tables 1 and 2).

Table 1. Actual Reserve Component Structure, 1962				
	Number	Percent Manning Level	Paid Drill Strength	Current Training Readiness (weeks)
1. Air defense (onsite) battalion (equivalent)	20½	84	9,200	0
2. Division forces	7	71	181,100	14–20
3. Units to reinforce Active Army	-----	71	129,158	4–21
4. Brigades	3	71	6,590	13–20
5. Support for other services	-----	65	16,252	13–19
6. Divisions	30	55–71	293,500	16–20
7. Training and operational base units	-----	55–71	64,200	2–8

Total paid drill strength:	700,000
Cost (in millions):	$771.3
Number of technicians (total):	20,770
Army National Guard:	17,554
U.S. Army Reserve:	3,216
Filler training (officers and enlisted personnel, 2 weeks):	32,000

Source: U.S. Congress, House of Representatives, Committee on Armed Services, Subcommittee No. 3, *Military Reserve Posture* (report), 87th Cong., 2d sess., August 17, 1962, 6668.

Table 2. Proposed Reserve Component Structure, Fiscal Year 1964				
	Number	**Percent Manning Level**	**Paid Drill Strength**	**Current Training Readiness (weeks)**
1. Air defense (onsite) battalion (equivalent)	16	85	7,231	0
2. Division forces	6	75–80	174,041	8
3. Units to reinforce Active Army	-----	80	137,402	4–8
4. Brigades	2	85	5,937	5
Brigades	9	75	30,947	8
5. Divisions with a special mission	2	70	26,006	12
6. Support for other services	-----	70	10,596	8
7. Divisions	21	50	146,092	20–34
8. Nondivisional units	-----	50	36,041	16
9. Training and operational base units	-----	100	66,539	1–4
10. Operational headquarters	8	100	1,168	-----
Total paid drill strength:			642,000	
Cost (in millions):			$781.2	
Number of technicians (total):			24,770	
Army National Guard:			17,554	
U.S. Army Reserve:			7,216	
Filler training (officers and enlisted personnel, 2 weeks):			100,000	
Source: U.S. Congress, House of Representatives, Committee on Armed Services, Subcommittee No. 3, *Military Reserve Posture* (report), 87th Cong., 2d sess., August 17, 1962, 6668–69.				

From April to July 1962, at the request of the full committee chairman, a subcommittee of the House Armed Services Committee conducted a "comprehensive inquiry into the defense posture of the Reserve components of our Armed Forces."[30] At the outset of the hearings, the subcommittee chairman, Representative F. Edward Hébert, indicated that the Department of Defense had agreed not to implement its proposed reorganization of the Army Reserve components until after the subcommittee had reached its own conclusions on this subject.[31] Following completion of the hearings, in August 1962 the subcommittee issued a report to the

---

[30] U.S. Congress, House of Representatives, Committee on Armed Services, Subcommittee No. 3, *Military Reserve Posture Hearings*, 87th Cong., 2d sess., April 16, 1962, 5400.
[31] *Military Reserve Posture Hearings*, April 16, 1962, 5400.

full committee that included an evaluation of the Department of Defense proposal. The report was critical of both the testimony presented by Department of Defense and army witnesses and the proposed reorganization plan, stating that the latter "was conceived by Army planners who were apparently more concerned with the problem of remaining within budgetary guidelines than with basically satisfying military requirements for increased readiness."[32] The subcommittee stated as a general observation that although it did not "question a military decision as to the number of personnel required by the Department of the Army for mobilization," it was "abundantly clear that our Army Reserve components require much more than a mere realinement of 'numbers' of personnel and 'division' organizations."[33] The subcommittee enumerated its specific reasons for opposing adoption of McNamara's plan:

- Its implementation will cause further deterioration of the morale of reserve units throughout the Army without significantly increasing readiness capability of the Army Reserve;

- It makes no provision to correct the present inability of the Army Reserve and National Guard to attract and retain trained and experienced senior enlisted personnel;

- It offers no concrete solution to the equipment problem which was so manifest during the recent mobilization; and

- It has been rejected by both the Reserve Forces Policy Board and Army Section 5 Committee which have the statutory responsibility of advising the secretary of the army and the secretary of defense on Reserve matters.[34]

In response to this critical reaction from Congress, Secretary McNamara scaled back his initial proposal, and in late 1962 he actually implemented a more modest plan to streamline and reorganize the Army Reserve components. The realignment involved realigning eight excess and low-readiness divisions into eight high-priority brigades. In 1962 Army Secretary Stephen Ailes testified before a subcommittee of the House Armed Services Committee that "the unneeded and excess units have been taken out the structure and the required new units have been added, so that it may fairly be said that the Reserve component structure has been modernized and brought into complete consistency with the Active Army we will have in the next fiscal year."[35] The

---

[32] U.S. Congress, House of Representatives, Committee on Armed Services, Subcommittee No. 3, *Military Reserve Posture* (report), 87th Cong., 2d sess., August 17, 1962, 6670.
[33] *Military Reserve Posture* (report), August 17, 1962, 6671.
[34] *Military Reserve Posture* (report), August 17, 1962, 6670.
[35] *Military Reserve Posture Hearings*, May 11, 1962, 5869.

rationale behind the restructuring was to increase combat readiness, achieve cost savings, and eliminate all units for which there was no military requirement.

In 1964, using essentially the same rationale, Secretary of Defense McNamara proposed merging all reserve components of the army under the management of the National Guard.[36] Congress rejected the proposal, in part because McNamara had neglected to consult with it and, in doing so, allegedly had violated the constitution.[37] The other reason for Congress's rejection is that the proposal faced intense resistance from the Reserve Officers Association.[38] Interestingly, McNamara's merger proposal was the exact opposite of the Gray Board's recommendation to eliminate the National Guard.[39]

The chronology of McNamara's ill-fated merger proposal is illuminating. On December 12, 1964, McNamara conducted a press conference and issued a press release announcing the realignment. The press release described the proposed reserve force structure as follows:

1) The force structure would consist exclusively of units for which there is a military requirement, including combat and combat support units together with base mobilization base units such as training divisions, garrison detachments and reception station augmentation detachments and would require a paid drill strength estimated at 550,000 men.

2) Five independent brigades would be added to the 11 currently in the structure, making a total of 16 independent brigades, which could be deployed as such or in association with other forces in the structure.

3) The entire force would be included in the structure for which the army purchases equipment; as a result equipment would be authorized for two additional divisions and five additional brigades.

4) The unit structure of the Guard and Reserve would be merged under the management of the National Guard.[40]

The press release indicated that such a realignment would result in increased combat readiness, streamlined management, and US$150 million in annual cost savings. The release even came with a detailed chart quantifying troop levels in various units before and after the proposed restructuring (see table 3).[41]

---

[36] William F. Levantrosser, "The Army Reserve Merger Proposal," *Military Affairs*, no. 3 (1966): 136.
[37] Levantrosser, 138.
[38] Brayton, 141.
[39] Doubler, 255.
[40] U.S. Congress, House of Representatives, Committee on Armed Services, Subcommittee No. 2, *Merger of the Army Reserve Components*, 89th Cong., 1st sess., March 25, 1965, 3557–3559.
[41] *Merger of the Army Reserve Components*, 3558.

Table 3. Comparison of Present [1965] and Proposed Reserve Component Structure						
	Present Structure				Realigned Structure	
Units for which there is a military requirement	Army National Guard	U.S. Army Reserve	Total	Manning level (percent)	Army National Guard	Manning level (percent)
Air defense	7,400	-----	7,400	85	7,400	85
Units to round out Active Army and Reserve (units will be added)	76,500	78,600	155,100	80	160,020	80
Brigades (now 11 brigades, to be increased to 16 brigades)	25,000	16,300	41,300	75–80	69,614	80
Mobilization base	2,600	66,600	69,200	75–100	69,200	75–100
6 division forces	118,000	64,100	182,100	75–80	189,860	80
2 special-purpose division forces	25,600	2,600	28,200	70	33,520	80
Support to other services	1,900	9,300	11,200	70	11,200	70
State headquarters	4,000	-----	4,000	100	8,500	100
Total	261,000	237,500	498,500	-----	549,314	-----

	Present Structure			Realigned Structure	
Units for which there is no military requirement	Army National Guard	U.S. Army Reserve	Total	Manning level (percent)	Army National Guard
Other divisions (21 divisions—15 Guard divisions and 6 reserve)	122,800	45,600	168,400	55–60	-----
Nondivisional units	15,450	16,300	31,750	55	-----
Command headquarters, divisional	750	600	1,350	-----	-----
Total	139,000	62,500	201,500		
Total	**400,000**	**300,000**	**700,000**	-----	**549,314**

Source: U.S. Congress, House of Representatives, Committee on Armed Services, Subcommittee No. 2, *Merger of the Army Reserve Components*, 89th Cong., 1st sess., March 25, 1965, 3558.

At the press conference McNamara elaborated on the above chart. He stated:

> At the present time we have an Army National Guard and an Army Reserve. The total strength authorized for the Guard is 400,000. For the Reserve 300,000. In each case the strength is broken down into those units for which there is a clear military requirement and those units for which there is no military requirement. There is a clear military requirement to support our contingency war plans for

six divisions and the associated support forces for units to round out the active Army, units that we would need in an emergency for sustained combat but which we do not require in peacetime and which we would not require to initiate combat. The total strength of these forces that are required to support our war plans is 498,000 men at the present time and they are manned to these levels, roughly 70 to 80 percent or 85 percent with a few at a hundred percent. In addition to the units requiring a strength of 498,000 men, we have 21 divisions, 15 in the Guard, 6 in the Reserve, for which there is no military requirement and for which no equipment purchases are authorized. Now the absurdity of the situation can be seen I think when you look at the total strength for these 21 divisions, 168,000 men…[There] is no equipment being purchased for these 21 divisions and quite clearly they are not manned in a way that would permit their deployment. As a matter of fact, we could start from scratch, organize the divisions, recruit the personnel, and train the men in less time than it would take to produce and distribute the equipment. So, these men are being wasted and the funds that are being expended to support them are being wasted.[42]

During the question and answer segment, McNamara clarified that following the implementation of his plan, the Army Reserve technically would continue to exist, but it would consist of individuals, not units. These individuals would participate in summer training and serve as trainees who could be called up in the event of a national emergency. In addition, he called attention to the benefit of reducing administrative overhead by eliminating a duplicative administrative structure.[43]

McNamara's decision to announce such a momentous change in policy in a press conference without prior consultation with Congress set off a firestorm among legislators. On February 22, 1965, a subcommittee of the House Armed Services Committee convened a hearing to confront him. During the hearing, Representative Hébert, the subcommittee chairman, addressed these remarks to McNamara: "I think you defied the law; you circumvented the intent of the Congress, and you have arrogated to yourself the powers that I don't believe you have, in what you have done in this area."[44] He informed Secretary McNamara that his actions violated the laws establishing the reserve forces and Congress's responsibility for maintaining militias

---

[42] *Merger of the Army Reserve Components*, March 25, 1965, 3576.
[43] *Merger of the Army Reserve Components*, March 25, 1965, 3577.
[44] *Merger of the Army Reserve Components*, March 25, 1965, 3572.

under Article I, Section 8, of the constitution.[45] On May 15, 1965, Secretary McNamara and Representative Hébert held a joint news conference, at which time the secretary announced he would submit legislation to Congress providing statutory authority for various elements of the department's realignment proposal. A few days later, Representative Hébert introduced H.R. 8243, a bill that included enabling enlisted men who had retired from the regular service to serve in the National Guard, permitting women to serve in the National Guard, and permitting the attachment of individual reservists to the National Guard for training.[46]

The introduction of H.R. 8243 did not mean, however, that Representative Hébert had acquiesced to Secretary McNamara's reorganization plan. At the conclusion of his subcommittee's hearings in August 1965, Hébert issued a statement that unequivocally opposed it:

> On the basis of extensive testimony received since March 15 by the subcommittee in both open and closed sessions, the subcommittee believes that the present proposal of the Department of Defense to merge the Army Reserve components is not in our national interest. The merger, as proposed by the Department of Defense, would result in an immediate and serious loss in the combat readiness of the affected Reserve units.[47]

In 1965 the Department of Defense and the nation's leadership were at odds regarding the role of reserve forces in Vietnam, with the Department of Defense in favor of deployment, and the politicians opposed. McNamara, following his setback in Congress, announced the creation of a Select Reserve Force, a 150,000-member joint Guard and Reserve force that trained diligently for service in Vietnam, but ultimately was never sent there.[48] In fact, the Select Reserve Force was abolished in 1969.[49] Also in 1965, McNamara recommended calling up 235,000 members of the National Guard and Army Reserve for service in Vietnam, but President Johnson, who was reluctant to alarm or antagonize the public, rejected the proposal.[50] Brigadier General Hal Nelson, Army Chief of Military History, called Johnson's surprise decision "a watershed in American military history."[51] As a result, according to Nelson, "the active force

---

[45] *Merger of the Army Reserve Components*, March 25, 1965, 3559, 3561–3562.

[46] *Merger of the Army Reserve Components*, Appendix III, xxxii and Appendix IV, xxxiv.

[47] "Subcommittee No. 2 News Release of August 12, 1965," *Merger of the Army Reserve Components*, 4454.

[48] Brayton, 141.

[49] Doubler, 257–58.

[50] "Assessing the Structure and Mix of Future Active and Reserve Forces," 31.

[51] Lewis Sorley, "Reserve Components: Looking Back to Look Ahead," *Joint Force Quarterly*, no. 36 (2005): 19–20.

was required to undertake a massive expansion and bloody expeditionary campaign without the access to Reserve forces that every contingency plan had postulated, and the Reserve forces—to the dismay of long-term committed members—became havens for those seeking to avoid active military service in that war."[52]

In September 1965, with the enactment of the fiscal year (FY) 1966 Department of Defense appropriations law, Congress formalized its repudiation of McNamara's plan. Pub.L.No. 89–213 appropriates funds for the Army Reserve and National Guard as separate components rather than as a merged force, and mandates drill strengths for each—270,000 personnel for the Army Reserve and 380,000 for the Guard.[53] Section 639 of this law prohibits the secretary of defense from transferring funds appropriated in the legislation to implement a "realinement or reorganization of the Army Reserve Components" without congressional approval, and stipulates that the mandated drill strengths would "cease to be effective" only if Congress enacted legislation implementing a reserve reorganization.[54] In August 1966, Representative Hébert introduced the Reserve Forces Bill of Rights and Vitalization Act of 1966, legislation that would have effectively permanently blocked a merger of the reserve components.[55] This bill was set aside in October 1966, when Congress enacted the FY 1967 Department of Defense appropriations law, Pub.L.No. 89–687, which reaffirmed congressional opposition to the McNamara reorganization plan by incorporating, in Section 639, language identical to that referenced above in Section 639 of Pub.L.No. 89–213.[56]

In 1967 McNamara assigned the National Guard the responsibility for combat and combat support; the reserves were left with a combat service support role.[57] The congressional response was the enactment of the Reserve Forces Bill of Rights and Vitalization Act.[58] Pub.L.No. 90–168 created a Selected Reserve "within the Ready Reserve of each of the Reserve components," including the Army Reserve and Army National Guard, consisting of organized units.[59] The conference report accompanying this legislation indicates that although the House bill "provided for permanent mandatory minimum strengths for the Selected Reserve in each of

---

[52] Sorley, 19–20.
[53] Pub.L.No. 89–213, 79 Stat 863, 864, September 29, 1965.
[54] Pub.L.No. 89–213, 79 Stat 879–880.
[55] H.R. 17195, 89th Cong.; 112 Cong. Rec. 23436, September 21, 1966.
[56] Pub.L.No. 89–687, 80 Stat 980, 997, October 15, 1966.
[57] Doubler, 255–56.
[58] Pub.L.No. 90–168, 81 Stat 521, December 1, 1967.
[59] Pub.L.No. 90–168, 81 Stat 521, 522.

the Reserve components," the Senate "was unwilling to establish minimum strengths for the Selected Reserve as a matter of permanent law."[60] The final language provides that the personnel strengths of each of the Selected Reserves of the reserve components are to be "authorized by law on an annual basis as a prior condition for the appropriation of funds for the pay and allowances for the reserve components."[61]

Pub.L.No. 90–168 is also significant because it created in statute the position of Chief of Army Reserve. The law amends Title 10 of the U.S. Code, providing a new section that stipulates: "There is in the executive part of the Department of the Army an Office of the Army Reserve which is headed by a chief who is the adviser to the Chief of Staff on Army Reserve matters."[62] The Chief of Army Reserve is appointed by the president, confirmed by the Senate, and must be in grade of brigadier general and above with a minimum of 10 years of commissioned service in the Army Reserve.[63]

In January 1968, President Johnson reluctantly ordered a limited reserve activation during the *Pueblo* crisis with North Korea.[64] However, as a result of his decision not to deploy reserves to Vietnam three years earlier, by this time it was demoralized, ill equipped, and ill prepared to mobilize. According to Lieutenant Colonel Lewis Sorley, U.S. Army (Ret.), "the result was a dismaying spate of class-action lawsuits by units contesting the legality of their mobilization."[65] A small number of reserve forces were sent to Vietnam in connection with the call-up, but by December 1969, they had reverted to reserve status.[66]

In April 1968, in response to the Tet Offensive in Vietnam, President Johnson issued Executive Order 11406 calling up to active duty 24,500 members of the National Guard and Reserves.[67] By one account, every unit that was recalled failed to meet minimum combat readiness standards.[68] By December 1969, more than 9,000 guardsmen had served in Vietnam.[69]

---

[60] H.R. Rep. No. 90–925 (1967).
[61] H.R. Rep. No. 90–925 (1967).
[62] Pub.L.No. 90–168, 81 Stat 521, 523.
[63] Pub.L.No. 90–168, 81 Stat 521, 523.
[64] "Assessing the Structure and Mix of Future Active and Reserve Forces," 32.
[65] Sorley, 20.
[66] Sorley, 20.
[67] Doubler, 259; 33 FR 5735, April 13, 1968.
[68] "Assessing the Structure and Mix of Future Active and Reserve Forces," 32.
[69] Doubler, 261.

TOTAL FORCE POLICY (POST–VIETNAM ERA)

A turnaround for reserve forces came during the post–Vietnam War era. In 1970 Secretary of Defense Melvin Laird introduced the Total Force Concept, which advocated the integration of active-duty and reserve forces into a "total force," with reserve forces responsible for augmenting their active counterparts. The Total Force Concept was motivated by a combination of Congressional cuts in defense spending and the pending abolition of the draft.[70] In 1973, the year the draft was abolished, Secretary of Defense James Schlesinger announced that the Total Force Concept had become the Total Force Policy.[71]

However, in 1975 Schlesinger began to express doubts about the just-implemented policy because in his words, "In the aftermath of Vietnam and the changeover to the all-volunteer force, we basically went too far in reducing our active-duty ground forces."[72] Some critics complained about a "hollow" army, which suffered from poor readiness in both active-duty and reserve forces.[73] In response, under the leadership of Army Chief of Staff General Creighton Abrams, the army adopted a Roundout Strategy, under which reserve brigades were used to "round out" active brigades. The reserve brigades had equal priority to the active units for equipment.[74] Abrams's practical implementation of the Total Force Policy through the Roundout Strategy gave rise to the so-called Abrams Doctrine, which was expressed by Abrams's frequent vow in the aftermath of Vietnam that "They're not taking us to war again without the Reserves!"[75] The Abrams Doctrine is popularly identified with the notion that under the Total Force Policy, "dependence on Reserve Components serves as an extra-constitutional tripwire on the presidential use of military power." According to this interpretation, General Abrams was determined "to maintain a clear linkage between the employment of the army and the engagement of public support for military operations."[76] The navy had initial misgivings about the Total Force Policy, but it fit the air force relatively well.[77] In 1982 Secretary of Defense Caspar Weinberger continued to support the Total Force Policy. Weinberger added the "First to

---

[70] "Assessing the Structure and Mix of Future Active and Reserve Forces," summary.

[71] "Assessing the Structure and Mix of Future Active and Reserve Forces," 32.

[72] "Assessing the Structure and Mix of Future Active and Reserve Forces," 34.

[73] James Jay Carafano, "The Army Reserves and the Abrams Doctrine: Unfulfilled Promise, Uncertain Future," Heritage Foundation, April 18, 2005, http://www.heritage.org/Research/NationalSecurity/hl869.cfm.

[74] Doubler, 299.

[75] Sorley, 22.

[76] Carafano.

[77] "Assessing the Structure and Mix of Future Active and Reserve Forces," 35–36.

Fight" principle for resource allocation, according to which "units that fight first shall be equipped first, regardless of component."[78]

ADJUSTMENTS FOLLOWING OPERATION DESERT SHIELD/DESERT STORM (POST–COLD WAR ERA)

In Operation Desert Shield (1990), which was designed to protect Saudi Arabia after Iraq had invaded Kuwait, Army Reserve mobilization was limited to combat support and combat service support troops.[79] The roundout brigades were not called up during the initial mobilization, but in November 1990 three such brigades were mobilized as part of a shift from defensive to offensive operations.[80] When actual combat commenced at the beginning of Operation Desert Storm on January 17, 1991, 23,000 Army National Guard units were stationed in Saudi Arabia. On the next day, President George H.W. Bush mobilized almost 1 million reservists for two years.[81] By the end of the conflict, 62,411 Army National Guard troops had been mobilized; of this number, 37,484 served on active duty in the Persian Gulf where they conducted the full range of combat, combat support, and combat service support activities.[82] In particular, the service of two reserve field artillery brigades—the 142nd of Arkansas and the 196th of Tennessee—validated the Total Force Policy in the view of the military.[83] However, the three Army National Guard roundout brigades saw no action during the conflict.[84] Specifically, the army declined to send the following roundout brigades to Saudi Arabia to support their active-duty counterpart divisions: the 48th Infantry Brigade (Mechanized) of Georgia, the 256th Infantry Brigade (Mechanized) of Louisiana, and the 155th Armored Brigade of Mississippi.[85] In a 1993 study, the General Accounting Office (GAO) found that forces of the National Guard and

---

[78] "Assessing the Structure and Mix of Future Active and Reserve Forces," 36.
[79] Doubler, 312.
[80] Doubler, 313.
[81] Doubler, 318.
[82] Doubler, 329.
[83] U.S Army, Center of Military History, *Department of the Army Historical Summary: Fiscal Years 1990 and 1991* (chapter 8, "Structuring the Force: The Army and Total Force Policy"), 104, http://www.army.mil/cmh/books/DAH SUM/1990-91/ch08.htm.
[84] Doubler, 332.
[85] U.S. Army Center of Military History, "Structuring the Force: The Army and Total Force Policy," 104.

Reserves supporting active-duty army troops during Operation Desert Storm displayed inadequate readiness.[86]

U.S. Army Reserve Command

As discussed earlier in this report, the position of Chief of Army Reserve was initially created in statute in 1967. In 1988 the chairman of the House Appropriations Defense Appropriations Subcommittee, Representative Bill Chappell, requested that the secretary of the army "look into the practicality of having the Chief of the Army Reserve also function as the Reserve component commander and of establishing a single reporting chain by consolidating the administrative units similar to the other Reserve components."[87] One year later, a U.S. Forces Command (FORSCOM) staff study concluded that the current U.S. Army Reserve command and control system did not need replacing.[88] Congress, however, continued to press the issue. In September 1989, Representative John Murtha, the new chairman of the House Defense Appropriations Subcommittee, wrote a letter to the army secretary, reminding the secretary that in its report to accompany the FY 1990 defense appropriations bill, the appropriations committee had "expressed concern about the command structure of the Army Reserve and directed the Secretary of the Army to begin actual planning to place command and control authority over the Army Reserve with the Chief of the Army Reserve."[89] The conference report accompanying the final defense appropriations legislation, Pub.L.No. 101–165, states that the conferees agree with the House that "the command, control and readiness of the Army Reserve would be improved by increasing the direct authority of the Chief of Army Reserve over these forces."[90] The conferees directed the secretary of the army "to prepare a plan [by March 15, 1990] to increase the role of the Chief of the Army Reserve, consistent with the command, planning and management responsibilities of the Chief of Air Force Reserve and Chief of the National Guard Bureau."[91]

---

[86] U.S. Congress, House of Representatives, Committee on Armed Services, Subcommittee on Military Forces and Personnel, *Reserve and Guard Effectiveness*, 103rd Cong., 1st sess., April 20, 1993 (statement of Richard Davis, Director, Army Issues, National Security and International Affairs Division, U.S. General Accounting Office).

[87] James T. Currie and Richard B. Crossland, *Twice the Citizen: A History of the United States Army Reserve, 1908–1995* (Washington, DC: Office of the Chief, Army Reserve, 1997), 318.

[88] Currie and Crossland, 320.

[89] H.R. 3072, 101st Cong.; Currie and Crossland, 322.

[90] H.R.Rep.No. 101–345, 14 (1989); Pub.L.No. 101–165, *Department of Defense Appropriations Act, 1990*, 103 Stat 1112, November 21, 1989.

[91] H.R.Rep.No. 101–345.

In October 1990, after numerous internal reviews of the issues involved, the army decided to establish a new U.S. Army Reserve Command as a major subordinate command of FORSCOM, to be fully operational by September 30, 1992. Congress was moving simultaneously toward a resolution of the command and control issue, and in the conference report to accompany the FY 1991 defense appropriations bill, the conferees stated that although the army's actions to establish an Army Reserve Command was a positive step, it did not go far enough:

> Command and control relationships between active and reserve forces, which are perceived by many as contributing factors to the relatively low readiness status of the Army Reserve, are not sufficiently changed in the current Army plan to provide actual command and control to the Chief of the Army Reserve.[92]

The conferees recommended that the Chief of the Army Reserve should command all nonmobilized reserve units, thus providing essentially the same command relationship as that afforded to the chiefs of the Air Force Reserve and Navy Reserve. The final law enacted by Congress in November 1990, Pub.L.No.101–510, Section 903, required the "establishment of a United States Army Reserve Command under the command of the Chief of Army Reserve. The Army Reserve Command shall be a major subordinate command of Forces Command."[93]

In its FY 1994 defense authorization act, Pub.L.No. 103–160, Congress amended the FY 1991 defense authorization act to stipulate that the Army Reserve Command "shall be a separate command of the Army commanded by the Chief, Army Reserve."[94] In addition, all forces of the Army Reserve were assigned to the commander in chief, U.S. Atlantic Command, instead of the commander in chief, U.S. Forces Command. The National Defense Authorization Act for Fiscal Year 1997, Pub.L.No. 104–201, repealed Section 903 of Pub.L.No. 101–510. The FY 1997 law amends Title 10 of the U.S. Code to add a new section 10171—U.S. Army Reserve Command. The law stipulates that "the United States Army Reserve Command is a separate command of the Army commanded by the Chief of Army Reserve."[95] The secretary of the army is authorized to prescribe the chain of command for the U.S. Army Reserve Command and to assign to it all forces of the Army Reserve in the continental United States other than forces assigned to the

---

[92] H.R.Rep.No. 101–923.
[93] Pub.L.No. 101–510, *National Defense Authorization Act for Fiscal Year 1991*, Title IX, 104 Stat 1485, 1620, November 5, 1990.
[94] Pub.L.No. 103–160, Title IX, 107 Stat 1736, November 30, 1993.

unified combatant command for special operations. All forces of the Army Reserve are assigned to the commander of the U.S. Atlantic Command.[96]

Total Force Policy Report

On December 31, 1990, the Pentagon's Total Force Policy Report to Congress, which was mandated by Pub.L.No. 101–510, the Fiscal Year 1991 Defense Authorization Act, recommended that active-duty forces "be able to deploy rapidly to trouble spots and to sustain themselves for the first thirty days with virtually no support from the reserve components," according to the U.S. Army's official historical summary for 1990–91.[97] The report recommended that active-duty and reserve forces complement each other rather than be mirror images of each other.[98]

The recommendations of the Total Force Policy Report and the decision not to deploy roundout brigades to the Persian Gulf during Operation Desert Storm led the Pentagon to phase out the Roundout Strategy after Operation Desert Storm. Instead, the army adopted a "Roundup Strategy," which established a new contingency corps prepared for immediate deployment to a war zone. This corps consisted entirely of five active-duty divisions, with an Army Reserve brigade assigned to each division for backup and subsequent deployment.[99] The implication of this new strategy was that in the post–Cold War environment the army was deemphasizing the role of reserve forces in its planning for immediate deployments.

Base Force

In fact, reserve forces were undergoing major shrinkage. From 1991 to 1995, the Army National Guard eliminated 70,000 positions.[100] The initial reduction was linked to the concept of the "Base Force," which was first discussed in 1990 just prior to the Persian Gulf conflict. Introduced by General Colin Powell, chairman of the Joint Chiefs of Staff, the Base Force was

---

[95] Pub.L.No. 104–201, Title XII, *Reserve Forces Revitalization Act of 1996*, 10 Stat 2422, 2689, September 23, 1996.
[96] Pub.L.No. 104–201, 10 Stat 2422, 2689.
[97] U.S. Center of Military History, "Structuring the Force: The Army and Total Force Policy," 104.
[98] Commission on the National Guard and Reserves, "Fact Sheet," February 26, 2007. http://www.cngr.gov/about-us.fact-sheet.asp.
[99] Doubler, 336.
[100] Doubler, 345.

defined as the "the minimum troop levels required among all of the uniformed services that still allowed the U.S. to maintain its superpower status and to meet world-wide responsibilities."[101] Additional reductions were set in motion in 1994, when the Department of Defense conducted a "Bottom-Up Review" of the Army National Guard and Army Reserves.[102]

Bottom-Up Review

The Bottom-Up Review was a restructuring plan that was linked to post–Cold War realities. Under the plan, the size of both the Army National Guard and Army Reserve would be reduced. The former would be given responsibility for combat, and the latter would be given responsibility for combat service support.[103] Delivering the coup de grâce to the Roundout Strategy, the Bottom-Up Review recommended that the Army National Guard consist of 37 brigades, including 15 enhanced brigades, which were subject to mobilization within 90 days.[104] In 1995 a RAND study concluded that the Bottom-Up Review force would provide an adequate combat force for two nearly simultaneous contingencies, but not an adequate support force for "anything beyond a single modest-sized contingency."[105] The reason was inadequate readiness.

Quadrennial Defense Review

In May 1997, the Quadrennial Defense Review embraced the need to create enhanced separate National Guard brigades, as recommended by the Bottom-Up Review, and "appropriate missions and size for our eight Army National Guard divisions."[106] It also called for additional reductions in reserve forces. However, as a result of resistance from reserve advocates, during 1997–2000 manpower reductions were limited to 3,000 at the Army Reserve and 17,000 at the Army National Guard.[107]

---

[101] Doubler, 335.
[102] Doubler, 348–350.
[103] U.S. Congress, House of Representatives, Committee on Armed Services, Subcommittee on Military Forces and Personnel, *Restructuring of the Army Guard and Reserve*, 103rd Cong., 2d sess., March 8, 1994, 12–13.
[104] Doubler, 350–51.
[105] Ronald E. Sortor, "Army Active/Reserve Mix: Force Planning for Major Regional Contingencies," RAND Arroyo Center, 1995, xv–xvi, http://www.rand.org/pubs/monograph_reports/MR545.
[106] U.S. Department of Defense, "Quadrennial Defense Review," May 1997, http://www.fas.org/man/docs/qdr/sec5. html; Major Donna Miles, USAR, "Reserve Components Under the QDR," American Forces Press Service, June 5, 1997, http://www.defenselink.mil.

MILITARY TRANSFORMATION (THE WAR ON TERRORISM)

Donald H. Rumsfeld, who served as secretary of defense during 2001–6, championed a policy of military transformation. This policy was aimed at transforming the military into a more agile force prepared to counter asymmetric threats from terrorist groups.[108] In testimony before the House Armed Services Committee in June 2006, Deputy Secretary of Defense Gordon R. England addressed the implications of military transformation for the National Guard. He stated that the National Guard, as an integral part of the total force, would be the beneficiary of improved procurement and resources and would be afforded more of a voice in decision-making.[109] In February 2006, the National Guard and Reserves accounted for about 30 percent of forces deployed in Iraq and Afghanistan, but General Peter Pace, chairman of the Joint Chiefs of Staff, announced that this share would be reduced to 19 percent in 2007 as active-duty forces would assume a greater role.[110]

Army National Guard and Reserve Transformation

In September 2002, Army Secretary Thomas E. White announced the Army National Guard Restructuring Initiative (ARNGRI), stating that this initiative would "improve the structure and training of the Army National Guard in order to better align it with other ongoing Army Transformation programs and the latest defense strategy." [111] Under this plan, two new organizations are introduced: mobile light brigades and multifunctional divisions. Also in 2003, Lieutenant General Steven Blum, chief of the U.S. National Guard Bureau, announced a plan to eliminate two-thirds of the Guard's state headquarters offices and reassign displaced personnel to units facing shortfalls. Instead of each state maintaining three separate headquarters, each would retain a single joint army and air force headquarters.[112] In addition to these steps, by 2005 the National Guard was preparing to boost readiness by:

---

[107] Doubler, 364–66.

[108] George Cahlink, "Rumsfeld Makes the Case for Military Transformation," *Government Executive*, January 31, 2002, http://www.govexec.com/dailyfed/0102/013102g1.htm.

[109] U.S. Congress, House of Representatives, Committee on Armed Services, *National Guard Enhancement*, 109th Cong., 2d sess., June 13, 2006 (statement of Gordon R. England, Deputy Secretary, Department of Defense), http://www.nexis.com.

[110] Lolita C. Baldor, "Role of Guard, Reserves to Lessen Overseas," Associated Press Online, February 8, 2006, http://www.nexis.com.

[111] "Army National Guard Restructuring Planned," *Army Logistician*, no. 1 (January/February 2003): 43.

[112] Katherine McIntire Peters, "Reorganizing the Guard," *Government Executive*, no. 9 (2003): 12.

- Moving from an alert-mobilize-train-deploy to a train-alert-deploy paradigm;[113]

- Providing such combat support units as "military police, chemical, information operations, and military intelligence" and "reaction forces to U.S. Northern Command (NORTHCOM) capable of dealing with chemical, biological, radiological, nuclear and explosive threats."[114]

- "Establish[ing] a joint continental United States (CONUS) communications support element (JCCSE) linking NORTHCOM, U.S. Pacific Command (PACOM), the Office of the Secretary of Defense (OSD), the Joint Staff, and other Federal and state agencies involved in [homeland security, homeland defense, and civil support]."[115]

At the same time, the Army Reserve was undergoing a similar transformation, consisting of the following:

- Moving from the alert-mobilize-train-deploy to the train-alert-deploy paradigm;[116]

- Scheduling deployments to increase predictability and restrict deployments to once per five years for a maximum of 270 days;[117]

- Eliminating units, particularly at headquarters, to maintain the remaining units at a minimum of 90 percent manpower;[118]

- Ensuring that soldiers are qualified in their military specialty and deployable;[119]

- Ending the practice of cross leveling (shifting manpower from one unit to another).[120]

Air Force Future Total Force

In 2005 the air force developed a plan for its total force structure, including a reorganization of the Air National Guard, over the next 20 years.[121] In 2007 the transformation of the Air Force Reserve from a strategic reserve mission to an operational war-fighting mission

---

[113] John C.F. Tillson, "Landpower and Reserve Components," *Joint Force Quarterly*, no. 36 (2005): 42.
[114] Tillson, 42.
[115] Tillson, 43.
[116] Tillson, 42.
[117] Tillson, 42.
[118] Tillson, 42.
[119] Tillson, 42.
[120] Tillson, 42.
[121] U.S. Government Accountability Office, "Defense Management: Fully Developed Management Framework Needed to Guide Air Force Future Total Force Efforts," GAO–06–232, January 31, 2006, http://www.gao.gov/htext/d06232.html.

was underway. Underpinning the transformation were three elements: the Total Force Initiative, the 2005 Defense Base Closure and Realignment Commission, and Program Budget Directive 720.[122]

The Total Force Initiative resulted in the creation of 10 air expeditionary force (AEF) units. Each AEF is prepared to deploy for 90 days every 15 months in response to contingencies in the United States or overseas.[123] Since September 11, 2001, AEFs and Air Reserve components have handled more than 75 percent of air interception flights over U.S. soil, an ongoing mission known as Noble Eagle. They also participated in Operation Iraqi Freedom.[124]

Regarding the base closure issue, in 2005 the U.S. Deparment of Justice issued an opinion on the proposal, stating that the Department of Defense may close or realign a National Guard base without the consent of the governor, contradicting one of the main arguments put forth by state lawmakers and National Guard leaders.[125] Nevertheless, the states have continued to challenge the Department of Justice opinion and to resist the base closure recommendations. The Air National Guard recommendations, which would strip all aircraft from 28 out of 89 flying units, has become the most contested issue in this base-closure round.[126] Along with base closures, Air National Guard personnel strength would decline by a net 3,500 positions from a base of 106,700.[127]

Program Budget Directive 720 involves the reduction of 7,700 billets in the reserves, to be accompanied by the elimination of 40,000 active-forces positions, over a three-year period.[128] The goal of the program is to free up resources for equipment modernization.[129]

Navy Active Reserve Integration

In 2004 Assistant Secretary of the Navy for Manpower and Reserve Affairs William A. Navas, Jr. was pursuing a policy of integrating the active and reserve navy.[130] He linked the

---

[122] Eric Hoffmeyer, "Proactive Force Planning," *Citizen Airman: The Official Magazine of the Air National Guard and Air Force Reserve*, no. 1 (2007): 14–15.

[123] Phillip S. Meilinger, "Airpower and the Reserve Components," *Joint Force Quarterly*, no. 36 (2005): 58.

[124] Meilinger, 58.

[125] Megan Scully, "States Say DOJ Opinion is Not the Final Word on Air Guard," *Congress Daily*, August 15, 2006, 3–4.

[126] William Matthews, *National Guard*, no. 9 (2006): 54.

[127] David B. Poythress, "Turbulent Times," *National Guard*, no. 4 (2007).

[128] "IMAs, Units to Share Reserve Personnel Reductions," *Air Force Link*, December 6, 2006, http://www.af.mil/news/story.asp?id=123034040.

[129] "IMAs, Units to Share Reserve Personnel Reductions."

Active Reserve Integration (ARI) policy to the "Naval Reserve Redesign" study completed in 2002 by Admiral William Fallon and Harvey Barnum. This study came up with 14 specific steps, more than half of which had already been implemented by 2004, to promote integration.[131] Still, the navy does not rely on reserve forces to the same extent as the army. According to Navas, only 23 percent of the navy's reserve force of 87,000 had been called up for duty in such recent operations as Operations Iraqi Freedom I and II, Enduring Freedom, and Noble Eagle. He attributed this relatively low percentage "in part to the fact that the Navy has managed its Reserve personnel resources in a prudent and judicious manner, mobilizing personnel only when absolutely necessary and using volunteerism to the maximum extent possible."[132]

In conjunction with ARI, in 2004 the chief of naval operations "approved personnel changes that would result in a net reduction of more than 16,000 reserve positions, a net increase of about 880 positions in the active force, and a net increase of about 450 civilian personnel positions."[133]

Marine Corps Total Force Structure Review

In 2004 the Marine Corps conducted a Total Force Structure Review.[134] In testimony before the Senate Armed Services Committee on February 10, 2005, General Michael W. Hagee, commandant of the Marine Corps, described the impact of initiatives spurred by the review as follows:

> In the reserve component these structure initiatives will increase the capability of Marine Forces Reserve Command to better respond to the Global War on Terror. We will establish an intelligence support battalion, a security/anti-terrorism battalion, and two additional light armored reconnaissance companies. We will also augment existing capabilities in the areas of civil affairs and command and control, and we are restructuring some reserve units to convert them into Individual Mobilization Augmentee

---

[130] William A. Navas, Jr., "Integration of the Active and Reserve Navy: A Case for Transformational Change," *Naval Reserve Association News*, no. 5 (2004).

[131] Navas, 15–17.

[132] Navas, 14.

[133] U.S. Government Accountability Office, "Force Structure: Assessments of Navy Reserve Manpower Requirements Need to Consider the Most Cost-effective Mix of Active and Reserve Manpower to Meet Mission Needs," GAO–06–125, October 18, 2005, http://www.gao.gov/htext/d06125.html.

[134] John W. Bergman, "Marine Forces Reserve in Transition," *Joint Force Quarterly*, no. 43 (2006): 26–28.

(IMA) Detachments—allowing more timely access to these Marine reservists to support contingency operations.[135]

BACKLASH AGAINST THE TOTAL FORCE POLICY

The military's growing commitment to the Total Force Policy, at a time when reserve forces are being pressed into repeated deployments to Afghanistan and Iraq in addition to the assumption of a new homeland security mission, has placed an unprecedented strain on reservists and their families. It has also led to the criticism that the distinction between active and reserve forces has blurred to the extent that it is now a distinction without a difference. In the view of Lieutenant Colonel Lewis Sorley, U.S. Army (Ret.), "What seems undeniable is that for whatever reason—fiscal, political, or strategic—the Nation is unwilling to maintain an active force that is adequate to current missions and operational tempo. As a consequence, Reserve forces not only supplement or reinforce the active force but often act as a surrogate for it. This stands the concept of Reserve forces on its head."[136]

Even before the terrorist attacks on the United States on September 11, 2001, Colonel James T. Currie, U.S. Army Reserves (Ret.), published an opinion piece in the *Army Times* entitled "If you overdeploy reserves, they're not really reserves."[137] In response, he received a flood of emails from army reservists complaining that they felt that recent deployments to Bosnia and elsewhere were neither essential to national security nor worth the disruption to their civilian

---

[135] U.S. Senate, Committee on Armed Services, *Defense Authorization Request for Fiscal Year 2006 and the Future Years Defense Program*, 109th Cong., 1st sess., February 10, 2005 (statement of General Michael W. Hagee, Commandant of the Marine Corps), http://armed-services.senate.gov/statemnt/2005/February/Hagee%2002-10-05.pdf.

[136] Sorley, 22.

[137] Commission on the National Guard and Reserves, *Hearing on Resourcing and Readiness, Employer and Family Support,* May 16, 2007 (statement of Dr. James T. Currie, "The National Guard and Reserve Today"), 2, http://www.cngr.gov/May%2015-17/currie%20testimony.pdf.

careers.[138] In May 2007, following continuous overseas deployments of reserve forces after September 11, 2001, Currie advocated a merger of the Army Reserve and Air Force Reserve into the National Guard, with the new expanded Guard focusing on homeland security.[139] Left unstated but implied by Currie's argument is the expansion of active-duty forces to compensate for the loss of integrated reserve forces available for foreign conflicts.

---

[138] *Hearing on Resourcing and Readiness, Employer, and Family Support*, 3.
[139] *Hearing on Resourcing and Readiness, Employer and Family Support*, 11.

APPENDIX A: TIMELINE FOR RESERVE COMPONENT REORGANIZATIONS

1947: The National Security Act of 1947 (Pub.L.No. 80–253) established the air force as a separate service, supported by the Air National Guard and the Air Force Reserve.[140]

November 1947: Secretary of Defense James Forrestal convened the Committee on Civilian Components, known as the "Gray Board."[141] The Gray Board was named after Assistant Secretary of the Army Gordon Gray.

June 1948: The Gray Board submitted its final report.[142] The Gray Board recommended the merger of the National Guard and Reserves into a federally controlled force called the "National Guard of the United States." This conclusion was based on the finding that the National Guard—with its dual state and federal allegiances—was not suitable for the Cold War. However, the National Guard and the National Guard Association of the United States successfully lobbied Congress against the Gray Board's recommendations.[143] The Gray Board also criticized the reserve forces for being long on experience but short on readiness because of their heavy reliance on World War II veterans.[144] Even though Secretary Forrestal convened the board, he did not endorse its recommendations.[145]

1948: The Selective Service Act of 1948 (Pub.L.No. 80–759) provided for a flow of manpower in the reserve units.[146]

September 1950: Four Army National Guard divisions were activated for deployment to Korea. Other reserve mobilizations followed.[147]

1951: The Reserve Forces Policy Board developed Department of Defense policies regarding reserve forces.[148]

July 9, 1952: The Armed Forces Reserve Act, which was designed to rejuvenate the reserve components, "divided them into three categories: ready, standby, and retired. The ready reserve was authorized a strength of 1.5 million. All [Air National Guard] units were placed in the highest priority category, the ready reserve—a position they had held in fact, if not law, since 1946. The legislation also allowed individual Guardsmen and Reservists to volunteer for active duty for routine peacetime operations and contingencies, thereby avoiding the political and

---

[140] Abbott A. Brayton, "American Reserve Policies Since World War II," *Military Affairs* 36, no. 4 (December 1972): 140.

[141] I.M. McQuiston, "History of the Reserves Since the Second World War," *Military Affairs*, Spring 1953, 23–27.

[142] McQuiston, 23.

[143] Michael D. Doubler, *Civilian in Peace, Soldier in War—The Army National Guard, 1636–2000* (Lawrence, Kansas: University Press of Kansas, 2003), 229.

[144] Brayton, 140.

[145] "Assessing the Structure and Mix of Future Active and Reserve Forces: Final Report to the Secretary of Defense," RAND National Defense Research Institute, 1992, 26–27.

[146] Brayton, 140; "Assessing the Structure and Mix of Future Active and Reserve Forces," 26.

[147] "Assessing the Structure and Mix of Future Active and Reserve Forces," 27–29.

[148] McQuiston, 25.

diplomatic risks of mobilizations."[149] The Armed Forces Reserve Act established the Coast Guard Reserve.[150]

1952: The Reserve Officers Personnel Act and Armed Forces Equalization of Benefits Act were introduced, but not enacted.[151]

August 9, 1955: "President Dwight D. Eisenhower signed the Reserve Forces Act of 1955, Pub.L.No. 84–305, into law. Among other provisions, the law required that all non-prior service enlisted recruits in the Air National Guard must undergo basic training by the Air Force beginning in Fiscal Year 1957."[152]

1957: The army imposed minimum training standards for all reserve personnel.[153]

February 1960: The air force adopted the "gaining command" concept of reserve forces management. "Its basic premise was that those major air commands which would fight Guard and Reserve Units during wartime would train and inspect them in peacetime."[154]

1961: President John F. Kennedy called up reserve forces in response to the Berlin crisis. The resulting mobilization went smoothly and was generally regarded as successful because it had the effect of deterring war. One important individual who did not share the consensus view was Secretary of Defense Robert McNamara (see next item).[155]

1962: Secretary of Defense McNamara recommended and implemented a plan to streamline and reorganize the Army Reserve components. The realignment involved realigning eight excess and low-readiness divisions into eight high-priority brigades. The rationale behind the restructuring was to increase combat readiness, achieve cost savings, and eliminate all units for which there was no military requirement. Secretary of the Army Stephen Ailes testified before the House Armed Services Committee that "the unneeded and excess units have been taken out the structure and the required new units have been added, so that it may fairly be said that the Reserve component structure has been modernized and brought into complete consistency with the Active Army we will have in the next fiscal year." The significance of this statement is that the same rationale was used two years later to justify the merger of the Army Reserve into the National Guard (see below).[156]

February 13, 1963: "The Air Force published AFR 45–60, 'Programming, Equipping, and Maintaining the Capability of the Air Force Ready Reserve Forces,' which changed the official objective of its reserve components from providing M–Day forces which required extensive

---

[149] Charles J. Gross, "A Chronological History of the Air National Guard and its Antecedents, 1908-2007," April 2, 2007, 34–35, http://www.ngb.army.mil/features/AF60th/ANG-CHRON_1908_2007.doc.
[150] Brayton, 143.
[151] McQuiston, 24.
[152] Gross, 42.
[153] Brayton, 140.
[154] Gross, 47.
[155] "Assessing the Structure and Mix of Future Active and Reserve Forces, " 30; Doubler, 251.
[156] U.S. Congress, House of Representatives, Committee on Armed Services, Subcommittee No. 2, *Merger of the Army Reserve Components*, 89th Cong., 1st sess., March 25, 1965, 3560–3561.

post-mobilization preparations for combat to ones that were immediately available for global operations when they were called to active duty."[157]

February 1964: "Secretary of the Air Force Eugene Zuckert approved 'in principle' a proposal for the 'eventual' merger of the Air National Guard and Air Force Reserve. The proposal was sent to the Air Staff for study but never implemented."[158]

December 1964: Secretary McNamara proposed merging all reserve components of the army under the management of the National Guard. Interestingly, McNamara's merger proposal, which Congress rejected, was the exact opposite of the Gray Board's proposal.[159]

1965: Following the defeat of his merger proposal, Secretary McNamara announced the creation of a Select Reserve Force.[160] However, this 150,000-member composite Guard/Reserve force, despite preparations for service in Vietnam, ultimately never served there. The Select Reserve Force was abolished in 1969.[161]

July 10, 1965: McNamara recommended calling up 235,000 members of the National Guard and Army Reserve for service in Vietnam. President Lyndon Johnson rejected the proposal.[162]

September 1965: Congress formally prohibited the implementation of McNamara's original merger proposal in the Fiscal Year 1966 Department of Defense Appropriations Act (Pub.L.No. 89–213).[163]

1966–1967: Congress again blocked adoption of the initial McNamara proposal in the Fiscal Year 1967 Department of Defense appropriations law (Pub.L.No. 89–687). McNamara later proposed and Congress approved another reserve reorganization, but without the merger proposal. Pub.L.No. 90–618, the Reserve Forces Bill of Rights and Vitalization Act, created a Selected Reserve within the Ready Reserve of each of the reserve components.[164]

January 25, 1968: President Johnson ordered a limited reserve activation during the *Pueblo* crisis with North Korea.[165]

February 1968: The National Advisory Commission on Civil Disorders, popularly known as the Kerner Commission, published a report that called for the National Guard to undergo training for crowd control and urban fighting. The report cited the problem posed by a predominantly white force being asked to quell black rioters.[166]

---

[157] Gross, 52.

[158] Gross, 53.

[159] William F. Levantrosser, "The Army Reserve Merger Proposal," *Military Affairs*, no. 3 (Winter, 1966): 135–47; Doubler, 255.

[160] Brayton, 141.

[161] Doubler, 257–58.

[162] "Assessing the Structure and Mix of Future Active and Reserve Forces," 31.

[163] Doubler, 255.

[164] Brayton, 141; "Assessing the Structure and Mix of Future Active and Reserve Forces," 30–31.

[165] "Assessing the Structure and Mix of Future Active and Reserve Forces," 32.

[166] Doubler, 263–64.

April 10, 1968: President Johnson authorized the activation of 25,000 reservists in response to the Tet Offensive in Vietnam. Every unit that was recalled failed to meet minimum combat readiness standards.[167]

1970: Secretary of Defense Melvin Laird introduced the Total Force Concept.[168] This initiative was linked in part to Congressional cuts in defense spending.[169]

1973: Secretary of Defense James Schlesinger heralded the Total Force Policy. Not coincidentally, the draft was abolished in the same year.[170]

1975: Secretary Schlesinger began to express doubts about the just-implemented policy. Under the leadership of Army Chief of Staff Creighton Abrams, the army adopted a "roundout" strategy, under which a reserve brigade would round out active brigades. In a separate initiative, support functions were transferred to the reserves. The navy also had misgivings, but the Total Force Policy fit the air force relatively well.[171] In January, Schlesinger rejected a proposal to merge the Air National Guard and Air Force Reserve despite the directive in the Department of Defense Appropriation Authorization Act, 1974 (Pub.L.No. 93–155) to study the possibility.[172] He stated that "the small savings realized by combining administrative headquarters could be offset by losses in combat readiness caused by a total reorganization of the Air Reserve component structure."[173]

1976: Congress gave the president authority to call to active duty up to 50,000 members of the Selected Reserve for up to 90 days without a declaration of war or national emergency.[174]

June 1982: Secretary of Defense Caspar Weinberger announced a "first to fight" policy for resource allocation: "Units that fight first shall be equipped first, regardless of component." He continued to support the Total Force Policy.[175]

1988: The reserves constituted more than one-half of army forces.[176]

August 2, 1990: Iraq invaded Kuwait. President George H.W. Bush soon responded with a slow, rolling call-up of reserves under an authority known as "Section 673b."[177]

---

[167] "Assessing the Structure and Mix of Future Active and Reserve Forces," 32; Doubler, 259.

[168] "Assessing the Structure and Mix of Future Active and Reserve Forces," summary.

[169] "Assessing the Structure and Mix of Future Active and Reserve Forces," 32.

[170] "Assessing the Structure and Mix of Future Active and Reserve Forces," 33–34.

[171] "Assessing the Structure and Mix of Future Active and Reserve Forces," 34; Doubler, 279–82.

[172] Pub.L.No. 93–155, 87 Stat 605,618, November 16, 1973. Section 810 of this statute directs the secretary of defense to "carry out a comprehensive study and investigation to determine the relative status of the Air Force Reserve and the Air National Guard of the United States," including the advantages and disadvantages of merging the Reserve into the Guard, or vice versa, or retaining both as separate entities.

[173] Charles J. Gross, *The Air National Guard and the American Military Tradition* (Washington, DC: National Guard Bureau, 1995), 120.

[174] "Assessing the Structure and Mix of Future Active and Reserve Forces," 35.

[175] "Assessing the Structure and Mix of Future Active and Reserve Forces," 36.

[176] U.S. General Accounting Office, "Army Force Structure: Future Reserve Roles Shaped by New Strategy, Base Force Mandates, and Gulf War," GAO/NSAID–93–80, December 15, 1992, 10, http://archive.gao.gov/d36t11/148167.pdf.

December 31, 1990: The Pentagon's Total Force Policy Report to Congress, which was mandated by the Fiscal Year 1991 Defense Authorization Act, recommended that active-duty forces "be able to deploy rapidly to trouble spots and to sustain themselves for the first thirty days with virtually no support from the reserve components."[178]

January 18, 1991: The day after the United States launched an air offensive against Iraqi troops occupying Kuwait, President George H.W. Bush authorized partial mobilization of the Ready Reserve.[179]

1992: The president's fiscal year (FY) 1992 budget proposed cuts in active-duty and reserve manpower.[180]

November 10–12, 1992: During the annual Air National Guard (ANG) senior commanders conference at Atlantic City, New Jersey, Major General Phil Killey, the ANG director, publicly unveiled his strategic vision for reshaping the ANG to meet the challenges of the post–Cold War era. The ANG would try to broaden its portfolio of flying missions to include acquiring bomber units as well as more airlift and tanker units in addition to seeking new missions like space for some of its support units. The Air Directorate, National Guard Bureau, would attempt to preserve all ANG flying units and protect the jobs of their personnel. To accomplish those goals, it would aggressively seek out alternative missions to rerole some ANG flying units, reduce the number of aircraft assigned to each unit, combine similar units at the same location if necessary, and, as a last resort, close down flying units."[181]

October 1992: Congress enacted the Army National Guard Combat Readiness Reform Act of 1992 as Title XI of Pub.L.No. 102–484, the National Defense Authorization Act for Fiscal Year 1993. This law establishes the objective of increasing the percentage of prior active-duty personnel in the Army National Guard by September 30, 1997 to 65 percent for officers and 50 percent for enlisted personnel. It also requires that each National Guard combat unit of the Army National Guard be associated with an active-duty component.[182]

April 20, 1993: The General Accounting Office (GAO) told Congress that the army had difficulty supplying ready support forces in the Gulf War.[183]

September 10, 1993: "Secretary of Defense Les Aspin issued his Fiscal Year 1995–Fiscal Year 1999 Defense Program Guidance which, among other things, resulted in ANG personnel taking over responsibility for manning First Air Force and its continental air defense mission from the

---

[177] "Assessing the Structure and Mix of Future Active and Reserve Forces," 40.

[178] U.S. Department of the Army, "Chapter 8, Structuring the Force: The Army and Total Force Policy," Historical Summary: FY 1990–1991, 1997, http://www.army.mil/cmh/books/DAHSUM/1990-91/ch08.htm#n1.

[179] "Assessing the Structure and Mix of Future Active and Reserve Forces," 50.

[180] U.S. General Accounting Office, "Army Reserve Forces: Applying Features of Other Countries' Reserves Could Provide Benefits," GAO/NSIAD–91–239, August 1991, 8.

[181] Gross, 101.

[182] Pub.L.No. 102–484, 106 Stat 2315, 2536–2542, October 23, 1992.

[183] U.S. Congress, House of Representatives, Committee on Armed Services, Subcommittee on Military Forces and Personnel, *Reserve and Guard Effectiveness*, 103rd Cong., 1st sess., April 20, 1993 (statement of Richard Davis, Director, Army Issues, National Security and International Affairs Division, U.S. General Accounting Office), 4.

Air Force in accordance with the recommendations of the Department of Defense's Bottom Up Review earlier that year."[184]

March 8, 1994: Based on a Bottom Up Review, the Department of Defense proposed a restructuring plan for the National Guard and Reserves. Under this plan, the size of both organizations would be reduced; the National Guard would be responsible for combat, and the Army Reserve would be responsible for combat service support. The restructuring was linked to post–Cold War realities.[185]

February 13, 1996: According to official Department of Defense documents, FY 1996 was the third year of a five-year plan to reduce and reshape reserve forces to meet strength levels established through the Bottom-Up Review.[186]

September 1996: Congress enacted the Reserve Forces Revitalization Act of 1996 as Title XII of Pub.L.No. 104–201, the National Defense Authorization Act for Fiscal Year 1997. This title revises "the basic statutory authorities governing the organization and administration of the reserve components of the Armed Forces in order to recognize the realities of reserve component partnership in the Total Force."[187] The law affirmed the U.S. Army Reserve Command as a separate command of the army, commanded by the Chief of Army Reserve, and established the Naval Reserve Force, Marine Forces Reserve, and Air Force Reserve Command as commands of, respectively, the Navy, Marine Corps, and Air Force.[188]

May 1997: The Quadrennial Defense Review addressed the need to create enhanced separate National Guard brigades, as recommended by the Bottom-Up Review, and "appropriate missions and size for our eight Army National Guard divisions."[189]

August 4, 1998: "The Air Force unveiled plans to reorganize more than 2,000 aircraft into 10 Air Expeditionary Forces (AEFs) to ease the strain of increased post–Cold War operations overseas. The AEFs would draw upon Air Guard and Air Force Reserve as well as active duty Air Force assets."[190]

September 2002: Secretary of the Army Thomas E. White announced the Army National Guard Restructuring Initiative (ARNGRI). Under this plan, two new organizations are introduced: mobile light brigades and multifunctional divisions.[191]

---

[184] Gross, 103.

[185] U.S. Congress, House of Representatives, Committee on Armed Services, Subcommittee on Military Forces and Personnel, *Restructuring of the Army Guard and Reserve*, 103rd Cong., 2d sess., March 8, 1994, 12–13.

[186] U.S. Department of Defense, Office of the Assistant Secretary of Defense for Reserve Affairs, "FY 1996 Reserve Component Reduction Plan," February 13, 1996, http://www.dod.mil/pubs/reduction/report1.html.

[187] Pub.L.No. 104–201, Title XII, *Reserve Forces Revitalization Act of 1996*, 110 Stat 2422, 2689, September 23, 1996.

[188] Pub.L.No. 104–201, 110 Stat 2422, 2689–2690.

[189] U.S. Department of Defense, "Quadrennial Defense Review," May 1997, http://www.fas.org/man/docs/qdr/sec 5.html; Major Donna Miles, USAR, "Reserve Components Under the QDR," American Forces Press Service, June 5, 1997, http://www.defenselink.mil.

[190] Gross, 112.

[191] "Army National Guard Restructuring Planned," *Army Logistician*, no. 1 (January/February 2003): 43.

February 26, 2003: "Thomas F. Hall, Assistant Secretary of Defense for Reserve Affairs, announced that there would be a 'rebalancing' of missions between the active duty and reserve components of the U.S. armed forces because of the high demands being placed on the latter."[192]

July 2003: Lieutenant General Steven Blum, chief of the U.S. National Guard Bureau, announced a plan in spring 2003 to eliminate two-thirds of the Guard's state headquarters offices and reassign displaced personnel to units facing shortfalls. Instead of each state maintaining three separate headquarters, each would retain a single joint army and air force headquarters.[193]

July 30, 2003: "Secretary of Defense Donald Rumsfeld signed a memo to the Chief, NGB directing the Bureau to examine ways to make the organization and the entire National Guard more relevant and accessible in the current national security environment."[194]

May 2004: In 2004 Assistant Secretary of the Navy for Manpower and Reserve Affairs William A. Navas, Jr. was pursuing a policy of integrating the active-duty and reserve navy. He linked the Active Reserve Integration (ARI) policy to the "Naval Reserve Redesign" study completed in 2002 by Admiral William Fallon and Harvey Barnum. This study came up with 14 specific steps, more than half of which had already been implemented by 2004, to promote integration. Still, the navy does not rely on reserve forces to the same extent as the army. According to Navas, only 23 percent of the navy's reserve force of 87,000 had been called up for duty in such recent operations as Operations Iraqi Freedom I and II, Enduring Freedom, and Noble Eagle. He attributed this relatively low percentage "in part to the fact that the Navy has managed its Reserve personnel resources in a prudent and judicious manner, mobilizing personnel only when absolutely necessary and using volunteerism to the maximum extent possible."[195]

November 17, 2004: "General John Jumper, Air Force Chief of Staff, testified before the House Armed Services Committee that 'There's nothing in any of our plans that reduces the manpower of the Air National Guard. That's point #1. We will be asking the Air National Guard to transition into more modern missions, along with the active duty. These more modern missions will include different things, like space operations, information operations, command and control, unmanned air vehicles.'"[196]

November 24, 2004: "The Secretary of the Air Force and the Air Force Chief of Staff signed a letter that directed MAJCOM commanders to provide plans no later than 17 January 2005 to test key initiatives for more closely integrating Guard and Reserve assets into active duty units and operations."[197]

August, 2005: The U.S. Department of Justice issued an opinion stating that the Department of Defense may close or realign a National Guard base without the consent of the governor,

---

[192] Gross, 129.

[193] Katherine McIntire Peters, Reorganizing the Guard, *Government Executive* 35, no. 9 (July 2003): 12.

[194] Gross, 130.

[195] William A. Navas, Jr., "Integration of the Active and Reserve Navy: A Case for Transformational Change," *Naval Reserve Association News*, no. 5 (May 2004), http://www.hq.navy.mil/mra/NavalReserveAssociation Article.pdf.

[196] Gross, 131.

[197] Gross, 131–32.

contradicting one of the main arguments put forth by state lawmakers and Guard leaders. The Air Guard recommendations, which would strip all aircraft from nearly two dozen units, has become the most contested issue in this base-closure round. The Department of Justice noted that the Guard functions both as a state militia and as a reserve component of the active-duty military. The states continued to challenge the Department of Justice opinion.[198]

February 2, 2006: General Peter J. Schoomaker, army chief of staff, denied widespread media reports that the president and Department of Defense were planning to cut the National Guard and its budget.[199]

November 16, 2006: The U.S. Northern Command (NORTHCOM), which was established in 2002, is increasingly reliant on reserve component forces, according to the Congressional Research Service.

May 16, 2007: J. Michael Gilmore, assistant director for national security at the Congressional Budget Office, testified before the Commission on the National Guard and Reserves on the following issues: past and projected operational tempos of the Army National Guard's combat units; the overstructuring of the Guard and the need for cross-leveling to deploy its units; equipment shortages; and recruiting, retention, and end strength. Cross-leveling refers to transferring personnel from one unit to another to bring the latter up to strength for deployment.[200]

---

[198] Megan Scully, "States Say DOJ Opinion is not the Final Word on Air Guard," *Congress Daily*, August 15, 2006, 3–4.

[199] Donna Miles, "Army to Ensure Reserve Components Fully Manned, Trained, Equipped," American Forces Press Service, February 2, 2006, http://www.defenselink.mil/news/newsarticle.aspx?id=14973.

[200] Commission on the National Guard and Reserves, *Hearing on Resourcing and Readiness, Employer and Family Support*, May 16, 2007 (statement of J. Michael Gilmore, Assistant Director for National Security, Congressional Budget Office, "Issues that Affect the Readiness of the Army National Guard and Army Reserve"), http://www.cngr.gov/May%2015-17/Gilmore%20testimony.pdf.

APPENDIX B: UNITED STATES CODE SECTIONS REQUIRING AMENDMENT IN ORDER TO EFFECT A MERGER OF THE ARMY NATIONAL GUARD WITH THE ARMY RESERVE AND THE AIR NATIONAL GUARD WITH THE AIR FORCE RESERVE

Title 10

Subtitle E, Part I – Organization and Administration

Chapter 1003 – Reserve Components Generally

> Section 10102 – Purpose of reserve components
> Section 10104 – Army reserve: composition
> Section 10105 – Army National Guard of the United States: composition
> Section 10106 – Army National Guard: when a component of the Army
> Section 10107 – Army National Guard of the United States: status when not in Federal service
> Section 10110 – Air Force Reserve: composition
> Section 10111 – Air National Guard of the United States: composition
> Section 10112 – Air National Guard: when a component of the Air force
> Section 10113 – Air National Guard of the United States: status whjen not in Federal service

Chapter 1005 – Elements of Reserve Components

> Section 10141 – Ready Reserve; Standby Reserve; Retired Reserve: placement and status of members; training categories

Chapter 1006 – Reserve Component Commands

> Section 10171 – United States Army Reserve Command
> Section 10174 – Air Force Reserve Command

Chapter 1007 – Administration of Reserve Components

> Section 10215 – Officers of Army National Guard of the United States and Air National Guard of the United States: authority with respect to Federal status

Chapter 1009 – Reserve Forces Policy Boards and Committees

> Section 10302 – Army Reserve Forces Policy Committee
> Section 10305 – Air Force Reserve Forces Policy Committee

Subtitle E, Part II – Personnel Generally

Chapter 1201 – Authorized strengths

Chapter 1203 – Enlisted members
Chapter 1205 – Appointment of reserve officers
Chapter 1209 – Active duty
Chapter 1211 – National Guard members in federal service

Title 32

Chapter 1 – Organization

Section 101 – Definitions – (3) National Guard; (4) Army National Guard; (5) Army National Guard of the United States; (6) Air National Guard; (7) Air National Guard of the United States; (12) Active duty; (19) Full-time National Guard duty
Section 102 – General policy
Section 104 – Units; location; organization; command
Section 105 – Inspection
Section 107 – Availability of appropriations

Chapter 3 – Personnel

Section 315 – Detail of regular members of Army and Air Force to duty with National Guard
Section 325 – Relief from National Guard duty when ordered to active duty

BIBLIOGRAPHY

"Army National Guard Restructuring Planned." *Army Logistician*, no.1 (January/February 2003).

"Assessing the Structure and Mix of Future Active and Reserve Forces: Final Report to the
      Secretary of Defense." RAND National Defense Research Institute, 1992.
      http://www.rand.org/pubs/monograph_reports/MR140.2.

Baldor, Lolita C. "Role of Guard, Reserves to Lessen Overseas." Associated Press Online,
      February 8, 2006. http://www.nexis.com.

Bergman, John W. "Marine Forces Reserve in Transition." *Joint Force Quarterly*, no. 43 (2006).

Brayton, Abbott A. "American Reserve Policies Since World War II." *Military Affairs*, no. 4
      (December 1972).

Cahlink, George. "Rumsfeld Makes the Case for Military Transformation." *Government
      Executive*, January 31, 2002. http://www.govexec.com/dailyfed/0102/013102g1.htm.

Carafano, James Jay. "The Army Reserves and the Abrams Doctrine: Unfulfilled Promise,
      Uncertain Future." Heritage Foundation, April 18, 2005. http://www.heritage.org/
      Research/NationalSEcurity/h1869.cfm.

Commission on the National Guard and Reserves. "Fact Sheet." February 26, 2007.
      http://www.cngr.gov/about-us.fact-sheet.asp.

Commission on the National Guard and Reserves. *Hearing on Resourcing and Readiness,
      Employer and Family Support*. May 16, 2007 (statement of Dr. James T. Currie, "The
      National Guard and Reserve Today"). http://cngr.gov/May%2015-17/currie%20testi
      mony.pdf.

Currie, James T., and Richard B. Crossland. *Twice the Citizen: A History of the United States
      Army Reserve, 1908–1995*. Washington, DC: Office of the Chief, Army Reserve, 1997.

Donnelly, Tom. "The Force We Have." *Armed Forces Journal*, June 2006. http://www.armed
      forcesjournal.com/2006/06/1813581.

Doubler, Michael D. *Civilian in Peace, Soldier in War — The Army National Guard, 1636–
      2000*. Lawrence, Kansas: University Press of Kansas, 2003.

Gross, Charles J. "A Chronological History of the Air National Guard and its Antecedents, 1908-
      2007." April 2, 2007. http://www.ngb.army.mil/features/AF60th/ANG-CHRON_1908_
      2007.doc.

Hoffmeyer, Eric. "Proactive Force Planning." *Citizen Airman: The Official Magazine of the Air
      National Guard and Air Force Reserve*, no. 1 (2007).

"IMAs, Units to Share Reserve Personnel Reductions." *Air Force Link*, December 6, 2006. http://www.af.mil/news/story.asp?id=123034040.

Levantrosser, William F. "The Army Reserve Merger Proposal." *Military Affairs*, no. 3 (1966).

Matthews, William. "Shrinking Fleet." *National Guard*, no. 9 (2006). http://www.nexis.com.

McQuiston, I.M. "History of the Reserves Since the Second World War." *Military Affairs*, 1953.

Meilinger, Phillip S. "Airpower and the Reserve Components." *Joint Force Quarterly*, no. 36 (2005).

Miles, Donna. "Reserve Components under the QDR." American Forces Press Service, June 5, 1997. http://www.defenselink.mil.

Navas, William A. Jr. "Integration of the Active and Reserve Navy: A Case for Transformational Change." *Naval Reserve Association News*, no. 5 (2004).

Peters, Katherine McIntire. "Reorganizing the Guard." *Government Executive*, no. 9 (2003).

Poythress, David B. "Turbulent Times." *National Guard*, no. 4 (2007). http://www.nexis.com.

Scully, Megan. "States Say DOJ Opinion is Not the Final Word on Air Guard." *Congress Daily*, August 15, 2006.

Sorley, Lewis. "Reserve Components: Looking Back to Look Ahead." *Joint Force Quarterly*, no. 36 (2005).

Sortor, Ronald E. "Army Active/Reserve Mix: Force Planning for Major Regional Contingencies." RAND Arroyo Center, 1995. http://www.rand.org/pubs/monograph_reports/MR545.

Tillson, John C. F. "Landpower and Reserve Components." *Joint Force Quarterly*, no. 36 (2005).

U.S. Army. Center of Military History. *Department of the Army Historical Summary: Fiscal Years 1990 and 1991* (chapter 8, "Structuring the Force: The Army and Total Force Policy"). http://www.army.mil/cmh/books/DAHSUM/1990-91/ch08.htm.

U.S. Army. Center of Military History. Office of the Chief of Military History. *American Military History* (chapter 26, "The Army and the New Look"). http://www.army.mil/cmh-pg/books/amh/AMH-26.htm.

U.S. Congress. House of Representatives. Committee on Armed Services. *National Guard Enhancement*. 109th Cong., 2d sess., June 13, 2006 (statement of Gordon R. England, Deputy Secretary, Department of Defense). http://www.nexis.com.

U.S. Congress. House of Representatives. Committee on Armed Services. Subcommittee No. 2. *Merger of the Army Reserve Components.* 89th Cong., 1st sess., March 25–September 30, 1965.

U.S. Congress. House of Representatives. Committee on Armed Services. Subcommittee No. 3. *Military Reserve Posture* (report). 87th Cong., 2d sess., August 17, 1962.

U.S. Congress. House of Representatives. Committee on Armed Services. Subcommittee No. 3. *Military Reserve Posture Hearings.* 87th Cong., 2d sess., April 16–July 13, 1962.

U.S. Congress. House of Representatives. Committee on Armed Services. Subcommittee on Military Forces and Personnel. *Restructuring of the Army Guard and Reserve.* 103rd Cong., 2d sess., March 8, 1994.

U.S. Congress. Senate. Committee on Armed Services. *Defense Authorization Request for Fiscal Year 2006 and the Future Years Defense Program.* 109th Cong., 1st sess., February 10, 2005 (statement of General Michael Hagee, Commandant of the Marine Corps). http://armed-services.senate.gov/statemnt/2005/February/Hagee%2002-10-05.pdf.

U.S. Department of Defense. "Quadrennial Defense Review." May 1997. http://www.fas.org/ man/docs/qdr/sec5.html.

U.S. General Accounting Office. "Army Force Structure: Future Reserve roles Shaped by New Strategy, Base Force Mandates, and Gulf War." GAO/NSAID–93–80, December 15, 1992. http://archive.gao.gov/d36t11/148167.pdf.

U.S. Government Accountability Office. "Defense Management: Fully Developed Management Framework Needed to Guide Air Force Future Total Force Efforts." GAO–06–232, January 31, 2006. http://www.gao.gov/htext/d06232.html.

U.S. Government Accountability Office. "Force Structure: Assessments of Navy Reserve Manpower Requirements Need to Consider the Most Cost-effective Mix of Active and Reserve Manpower to Meet Mission Needs." GAO–06–125, October 18, 2005. http://www.gao.gov/htext/d06125.html.